PIANO • VOCAL • GUITAR

RETROSPECTIVE
THE BEST OF
BUFFALO SPRINGFIELD

ISBN 978-1-4768-7436-4

HAL•LEONARD®
CORPORATION
7777 W. BLUEMOUND RD. P.O. BOX 13819 MILWAUKEE, WI 53213

Visit Hal Leonard Online at
www.halleonard.com

RETROSPECTIVE THE BEST OF BUFFALO SPRINGFIELD

CONTENTS

FOR WHAT IT'S WORTH

Words and Music by
STEPHEN STILLS

Slow Rock beat

There's some-thing hap-pen-ing here.__

What it is ain't ex-act-ly clear.__

There's a man with a gun o-ver there__

MR. SOUL

Words and Music by
NEIL YOUNG

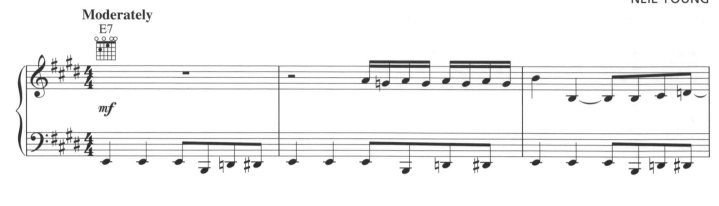

Oh, hel - lo, _____ Mis - ter Soul, __ I dropped __ by to pick up a rea -

- son for the thought __ that I caught __ that my head __

_____ is the e - vent of the sea - son. Why in crowds __

let her.

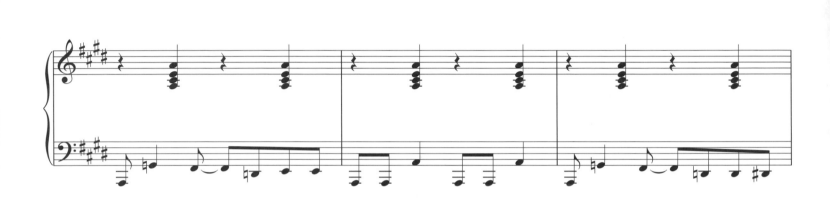

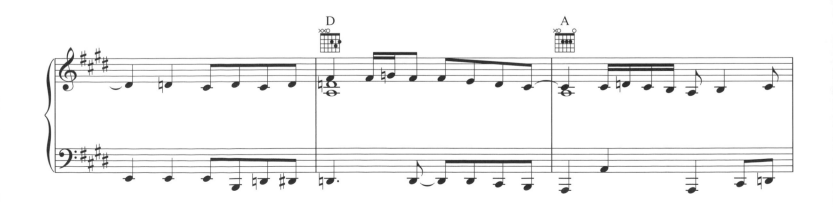

SIT DOWN I THINK I LOVE YOU

Words and Music by
STEPHEN STILLS

It's not much I'm ask - in' of ___ you. Just to please give

me a try. ___

KIND WOMAN

Words and Music by
RICHIE FURAY

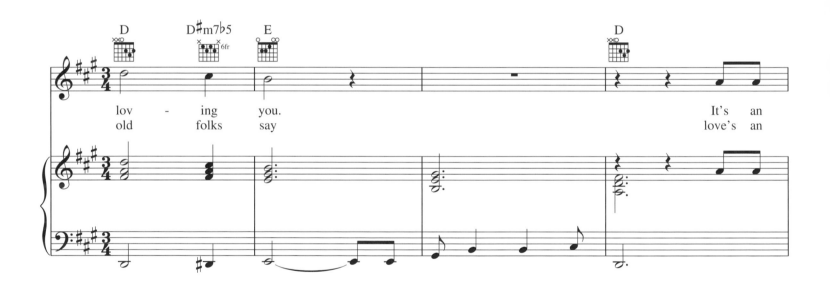

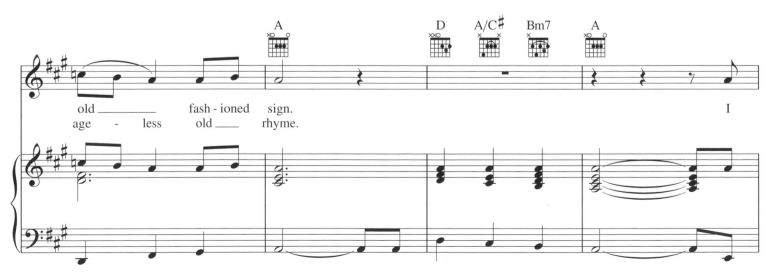

BLUEBIRD

Words and Music by
STEPHEN STILLS

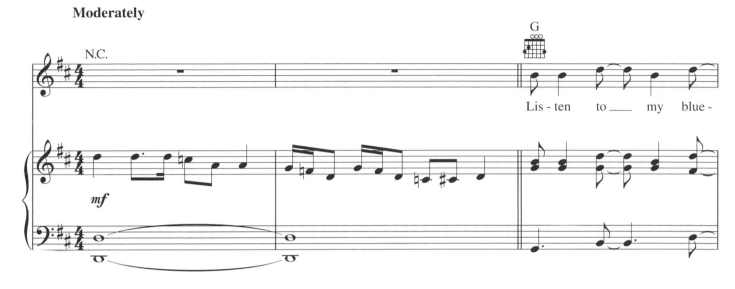

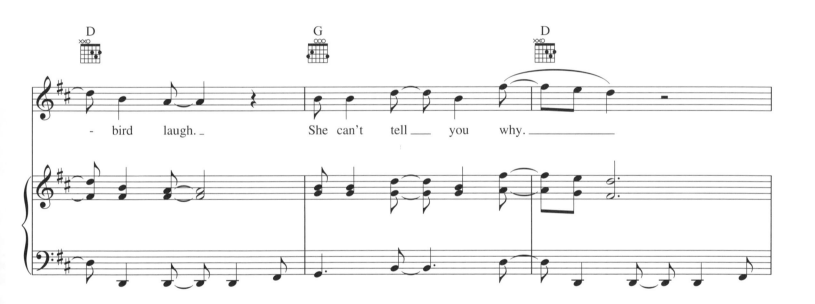

cry - in',   just   cry -   in'.

There she sits ___ a - loft ___ a perch, ___ strang - est col - or blue. ___

___ Fly - in' is ___ for - got - ten now. ___

Thinks on - ly of you, _____ just

you, _____ oh, _____ yeah.

So get all ___ those blues, _ must be a thou - sand hues ___ and be just

dif - f'rent - ly used, _ you just know. You sit there mes - mer - ized ___ by the

depth of her eyes that you can't cat - e - gor - ize.___ She got soul, she got

soul, she got soul, she got soul._____

Do you ___ think _____ she

loves you? _____ Do you ___ think _____

___ at all? _____

ON THE WAY HOME

Words and Music by
NEIL YOUNG

NOWADAYS CLANCY CAN'T EVEN SING

Words and Music by
NEIL YOUNG

BROKEN ARROW

Words and Music by
NEIL YOUNG

The lights turned on and the
Eigh - teen years of A -
streets were lined for the

cur - tain fell down.   And   when it was o - ver, it
mer - i - can dream.   He   saw that his broth - er had
wed - ding par - ade.   The   Queen wore the white of the

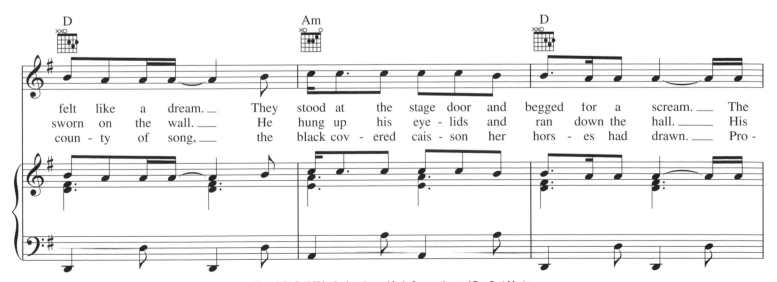

felt like a dream. ___ They stood at the stage door and begged for a scream. ___ The
sworn on the wall. ___ He hung up his eye - lids and ran down the hall. ___ His
coun - ty of song, ___ the black cov - ered cais - son her hors - es had drawn. ___ Pro -

a - gents had paid for the black lim - ou - sine ___ that wait - ed out - side in the
moth - er had told him a trip was a fall. ___ And don't men - tion ba - bies at
tect - ed her King from the sun rays of dawn. ___ They mar - ried for peace and were

rain.
all.   Did you see ___ them?   Did you
gone.

see ___ them?

Did you see them   in the riv - er?

ROCK AND ROLL WOMAN

Words and Music by
STEPHEN STILLS

Could it ____ be she don't have ____ to try. ____

42

D.C. al Coda

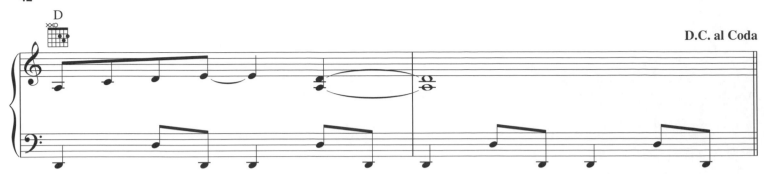

CODA

hard _____ to find. _____

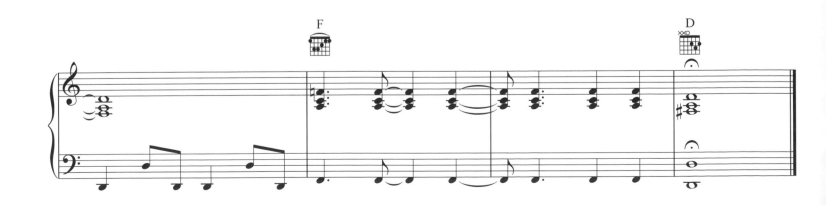

I AM A CHILD

Words and Music by
NEIL YOUNG

I am a child, ___
You are a man, ___

I last a while. ___
you un - der - stand. ___

GO AND SAY GOODBYE

Words and Music by
STEPHEN STILLS

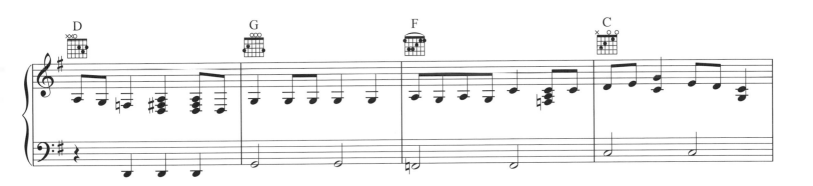

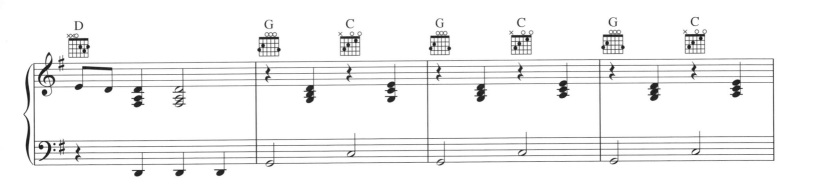

You ask me to read ___ this let- ter, that you wrote ___
___ the fault ___ was yours ___ and you real-
know the pain ___ is dou- ble, but for her ___

48

EXPECTING TO FLY

Words and Music by
NEIL YOUNG

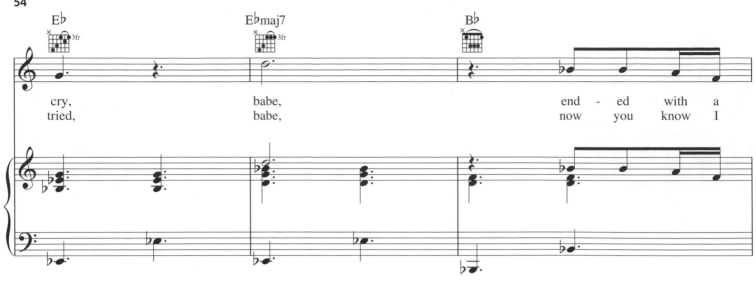

cry,   babe,   end - ed with a
tried,   babe,   now you know I

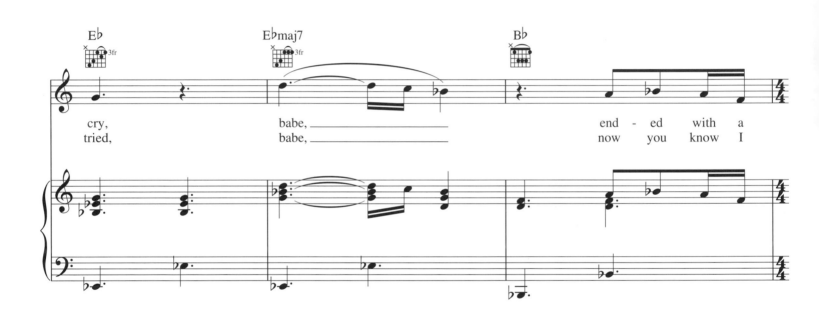

cry,   babe, _____   end - ed with a
tried,   babe, _____   now you know I

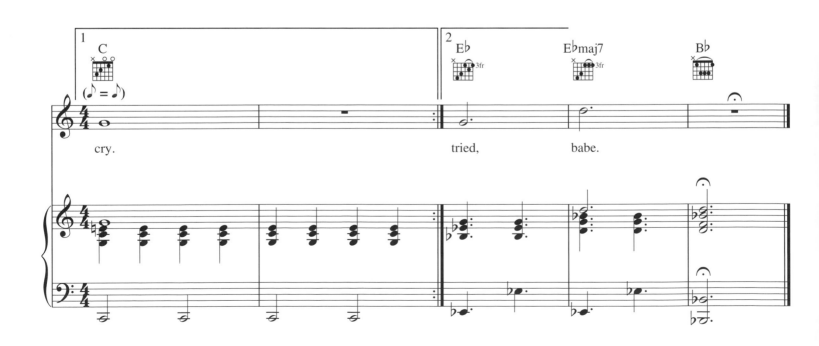

cry.   tried, babe.